UNIFORMS WORN DURING 1740-1760

Uniforms Worn During 1740–1760

Illustrated by
LT. COL. FRANK WILSON
with descriptive text by
ARTHUR KIPLING

CHARLES KNIGHT & CO. LTD.
LONDON
1974

CHARLES KNIGHT & CO. LTD.
11/12 Bury Street, London, EC3A 5AP
Dowgate Works, Douglas Road, Tonbridge, Kent.

Printed in Great Britain by
List and Print Services Ltd.,
a member of the Brown Knight & Truscott Group
London and Tonbridge

ISBN 0 85314 204 1

Contents

Introduction   1

The War of the Austrian Succession

King George II at Dettingen   3
British and Allied Cavalry at Dettingen   4
Horse Grenadier Guards   9
Officer and Gunner, Royal Artillery, 1743   10
Gun Team, The Royal Regiment of Artillery   12
The British Infantry at Dettingen   14
British and Allied Infantry, 1743   16
The Highland Regiment   22
Lord Charles Hay at Fontenoy   24
Arms of the British Soldier, 1743-60   27
The French Cavalry, 1743-45   28
French Infantry, 1743-45   31

The Seven Years' War

Dragoons Marching Order, 1751   34
Farriers   35
Light Troops   36
British Cavalry in the Seven Years' War   38
Artillery in the Seven Years' War   42
Roses at Minden   42
British Infantry in the Seven Years' War   44
Drummers and Fifers   47
The Marquis of Granby   49
A Camp Scene   50
The German Contingents in the Allied Army   51
The Lieb Garde of Hanover   53
The French Cavalry at Minden   55
French Infantry at Minden   58

Illustrations

Fig.

1.	King George II leads his army on foot	3
2.	2nd Troop of Horse Grenadier Guards, 1743	9
3.	Officer and Gunner, Royal Artillery, 1743	11
4.	Gun Team and Flag Gun, 1743	13
5.	Uniforms of British Infantry at Dettingen (1)	14
6.	Uniforms of British Infantry at Dettingen (2)	15
7.	Austrian Infantry, 1743	17
8.	The Highland Regiment, 1745	23
9.	Lord Charles Hay at Fontenoy	25
10.	Arms of the British Soldier	26
11.	Marching Order, 7th or Queen's Own Dragoons, 1751	34
12.	Farrier, 11th Dragoons, 1751	36
13.	Private, Light Troop, 11th Dragoons	37
14.	A Rose for Minden	43
15.	Fifer, 1745, Drummer, 1751, Drummers' cap, 1751, Fife Case, 1745	48
16.	"Going for it, bald-headed"	49
17.	A Camp Scene	50
18.	The Lieb Garde of Hanover	54

Plates

1.	British and Allied Cavalry, 1743-45	5
2.	British and Allied Infantry, 1743-45	21
3.	French Cavalry, 1743-45	30
4.	French Infantry, 1743-45	33
5.	British and Allied Cavalry, 1759-60	39
6.	British and Allied Infantry, 1759-60	46
7.	French Cavalry, 1759-60	57
8.	French and Allied Units, 1759	60

Introduction

During the period 1740-1760 Britain was involved in the War of the Austrian Succession, 1740-1748, and the Seven Years' War, 1756-1763, and this book illustrates some of the uniforms worn during these eventful years.

Both campaigns produced notable feats of arms. At Dettingen[1] June 27th, 1743, George II was the last King of England to take part in a battle. When the engagement was over he revived the creation of Knights banneret in the field. Amongst those so honoured were the Commander in Chief, Lord Stair and Trooper Thomas Brown of The King's Own Regiment of Dragoons who though severely wounded had shown great gallantry in rescuing the Regimental Standard which had been taken by the French.

Fontenoy, May 11th, 1745, was not a victory, but the courage evinced by the British troops won the admiration of their opponents. The fighting qualities of the Irish regiments in the French service played a big part in the ultimate result.

Probably the best known battle during the Seven Years' War is that of Minden[2] fought on the 1st August, 1759, where, owing to a mistaken interpretation of an order six British and two Hanoverian regiments advanced alone against the mass of French Cavalry.

The action of Emsdorf, 16th July, 1760, is famous for the achievement of the 15th Light Dragoons when they defeated and captured five battalions of Foot with three Colours and nine guns, and the British Cavalry generally excelled themselves at the battle of Warburg, 31st July, 1760.

It is not intended in this series to show all the various types of uniform worn by the British troops and their allies and those of their opponents, but to give sufficient detail so that Wargamers can dress their models in the appropriate costume for the battles they are enacting.

1   Dettingen 1743 by Michael Orr   2   Minden 1760 by Howard N. Cole
(both in Knight's Battles for Wargamers)

The author and illustrator would like to express their deep debt of gratitude to the memory of their old friend the late Cecil C. P. Lawson without whose classics on the dress of the British Army, these books would have been impossible.

We also wish to acknowledge the help given by the Marquess of Cambridge G.C.V.O. who kindly supplied details of the French, Austrian and Hanoverian uniforms.

KING GEORGE II AT DETTINGEN

A burst of fire startled the King's horse which bolted to the rear of the army. It was stopped and the King dismounted and moved on foot to a place beside the Hanoverian battalions on the right flank.

Fig.1. King George II leads his army on foot

Later the King's son the Duke of Cumberland had a similar experience but his horse carried him towards the French Cavalry. Fortunately he was able to regain control and return to his own lines, but he was mistaken for a French cavalryman by an Austrian Officer who shot him in the thigh.

BRITISH AND ALLIED CAVALRY AT DETTINGEN

The British had six regiments of Horse and six of Dragoons at Dettingen and details of their dress and appointments are shown in the table on pages 6 and 7.

On the colour plate the mounted figures are left to right a private of a Regiment of Horse. Note that he wears two cross-belts. In the centre a private of the Royal Regiment of North British Dragoons, the only regiment to have white equipment, the rest being light buff, and on the right a private gentleman of the 4th Troop of Life Guards of Horse. The 4th Troop had blue stripes on the carbine belt, the 1st having red, the 2nd white and the 3rd yellow.

The dismounted men in the foreground are on the left a Grenadier of the Regiment of Ligne of the Austrian Army, next a private of a regiment of Dragoons. He wears only one cross-belt. Dragoons were regarded as inferior to Horse and frequently fought on foot with every tenth man a Horse holder.

The third figure is that of a grenadier of the Regiment of Adelepsen of the Hanoverian Army. When mounted his shabraque and holster caps would be blue with a border of crimson and white.

The final figure is that of an officer of cavalry. As he has silver lace his hat is also edged with silver. Gold laced regiments had gold lace on the hat.

The Hanoverian Army supplied eight regiments of Horse and five of Dragoons and these were dressed as follows:

HORSE

Garde du Corps: Red coat and cuffs, blue lining, silver lace and belt, straw coloured waistcoat.

Lieb Regiment: White coat, yellow facings, white buttons.

von Schultzen: White coat, blueish green facings, yellow buttons.

von Hammerstein: White coat, dark green facings, yellow buttons.

Montigni: White coat, blueish green facings, white buttons.

British and Allied Cavalry, 1743-45

HORSE

REGIMENT	FACINGS	WAISTCOAT	BREECHES
3rd Troop of Life Guards of Horse	Blue	Light Buff	Buff
4th Troop of Life Guards of Horse	Blue	Light Buff	Buff
2nd or Scotch Troop of Horse Grenadier Guards	Blue	Buff	Buff
The Royal Regiment of Horse Guards	Red Uniform Blue	Red	Blue
The King's Own Regiment of Horse (Honeywood's)	Blue	Blue	Blue
The Eighth Horse (Ligonier's)	Yellow	Yellow	Yellow

DRAGOONS

REGIMENT	FACINGS	WAISTCOAT	BREECHES
The Royal Regiment of Dragoons (Hanley's)	Blue	Blue	Red
The Royal Regiment of North British Dragoons	Blue	Blue	Blue
The King's Own Regiment of Dragoons (Bland's)	Light Blue	Light Blue	Light Blue
Lt.Gen.Rich's Regiment of Dragoons	Green	Green	Green
The Earl of Stair's Regiment of Dragoons	Yellow	Yellow	Red
The Queen's Own Regiment of Dragoons (Cope's)	White	White	White

AT DETTINGEN – 27th JUNE, 1743

CLOAK	FLASK CORD	HAT LACE	HOUSINGS AND HOLSTER CAPS	TITLE IN 1920
Red, Lined Blue	Carbine Belt Yellow Stripe	Gold	Gold Lace Yellow Stripe	Disbanded 1746
Red, Lined Blue	Carbine Belt Blue Stripe	Gold	Gold Lace Blue Stripe	Disbanded 1746
Red, Lined Blue	Red	Yellow	Red, Blue Centre Stripe edged Yellow	2nd Life Guards
Blue, Lined Red	Red	Yellow	Red, White and Yellow Embroidery	Royal Horse Guards (The Blues)
Red, Lined Blue	Blue	Yellow	Red, Yellow and White Embroidery	1st King's Dragoon Guards
Red, Lined Yellow	Yellow and Buff	White	White, Red and Dark Blue Embroidery	7th Dragoon Guards (Princess Royal's)
Red and Blue	Blue	Yellow	Blue, White and Yellow Embroidery	1st The Royal Dragoons
Red and Blue	Red	Yellow	Red, Yellow and Green Foliage	The Royal Scots Greys (2nd Dragoons)
Red and Light Blue	Blue	Yellow	Red and Yellow Embroidery	3rd The King's Own Hussars
Red and Green	Buff	White	Green, White and Red Embroidery	4th Queen's Own Hussars
Red and Yellow	Buff	White	Yellow, Red and Black Embroidery	The Inniskillings (6th Dragoons)
Red and White	White	White	White, Red, Blue and Yellow Embroidery	7th Queen's Own Hussars

Bremer: White coat dark blue facings, yellow buttons, straw
coloured waistcoat.
Wreden: White coat, red facings, yellow buttons, straw coloured
collar.
Bullow: White coat, red facings, white buttons.

DRAGOONS

Pontietin: White coat, red facings, yellow buttons, straw coloured waistcoat.
Wendt: White coat and buttons, red facings.
Bussche: White coat, dark blue facings, yellow buttons, straw
coloured collar.
Adelepsen: White coat, light blue facings, white buttons, light
straw coloured collar.
Grenadiers à Cheval: Red coat and lining, black lapel and cuffs,
straw coloured waistcoat, grenadier cap with black front.

The Austrian Army contributed two regiments of Dragoons.
de Ligne: Blue coat, red facings, yellow buttons.
Limberg Styrum: Red coat, blue facings, white buttons.

HORSE GRENADIER GUARDS

A troop of Horse Grenadier Guards was raised in 1678 and soon after 1684 a 2nd or Scotch troop was formed. This regiment was at Dettingen and the illustration shows the uniform worn at that date.

Fig.2. 2nd Troop of Horse Grenadier Guards, 1743

The badge on the cloth cap is embroidered: a yellow Royal Cypher "GR" on red ground within the Garter and surmounted by a crown. The front of the cap is red embroidered in white, with turn up in blue bearing a thistle. A red tuft at the top.

Coat is red, no lapels, white lace loops and buttons. White shoulder knot on right arm, blue cuffs and turnbacks. Breeches pale buff with white knee pieces.

The flask cord is red (the 1st Troop of Horse Grenadier Guards had blue flask cords and blue tufts).

The horse is probably a brown bay or black and the firelock is in the position "advance your muskets", the butt resting in a bucket on the offside.

Housings and Holster Caps red, edged yellow with blue central stripe. Within the border the Royal Cypher, Garter and Crown.

At top right is shown the cartridge pouch and a powder horn supported by the red flask cord.

OFFICER AND GUNNER, ROYAL ARTILLERY, 1743

The officer wears a blue coat with blue lapels and brass buttons. The coat has red cuffs and red turnbacks on the skirt. His hat is trimmed with gold lace and he wears white spatter-dashes.

A crimson sash is worn over the left shoulder. This was long and broad and had a hole at each end so that a pole could be run through and convert it into a hammock to carry the officer if he was wounded.

He also wears a white buff waistbelt on which is a cartouche box embellished with a gold crown on red cloth.

His arms are a long brass-hilted sword and a fusil. Fusils were discontinued in 1759.

Fig.3. Officer and Gunner, Royal Artillery, 1743

The Non-Commissioned Officers, Gunners and Matrosses were dressed in blue coats with scarlet half-lapels, scarlet cuffs and turn backs, slashed sleeves with five buttons. Blue waistcoats and breeches.

Sergeants had gold lace on their hats, other ranks a narrow edging of gold.

Sergeants, Corporals and Bombardiers were armed with halberds and brass hilted swords.

Gunners carried linstocks, these were two feet longer than the halberd. Over the left shoulder was carried a powder horn for priming.

Matrosses were armed with muskets and bayonets.

GUN TEAM, THE ROYAL REGIMENT OF ARTILLERY, 1743

The drivers attached to the Train of Artillery were civilians who wore white frocks with the letters "G.R." in red on their backs.

COMMANDEERED

Last year he drew the harvest home
Along the winding upland lane,
The children twisted marigolds
And clover flowers to deck his mane.
Last year he drew the harvest home.

Today, with puzzled, patient face,
With ears a-droop and weary feet
He marches to the sound of drums
And draws the gun along the street.
Today he draws the guns of war!

L. G. Moberley.

(Reproduced by permission of *Punch.*)

The flag-gun was used to indicate the headquarters of the Artillery, and also the position of those of the General Commanding in the field.

Fig.4. Gun Team and Flag Gun, 1743

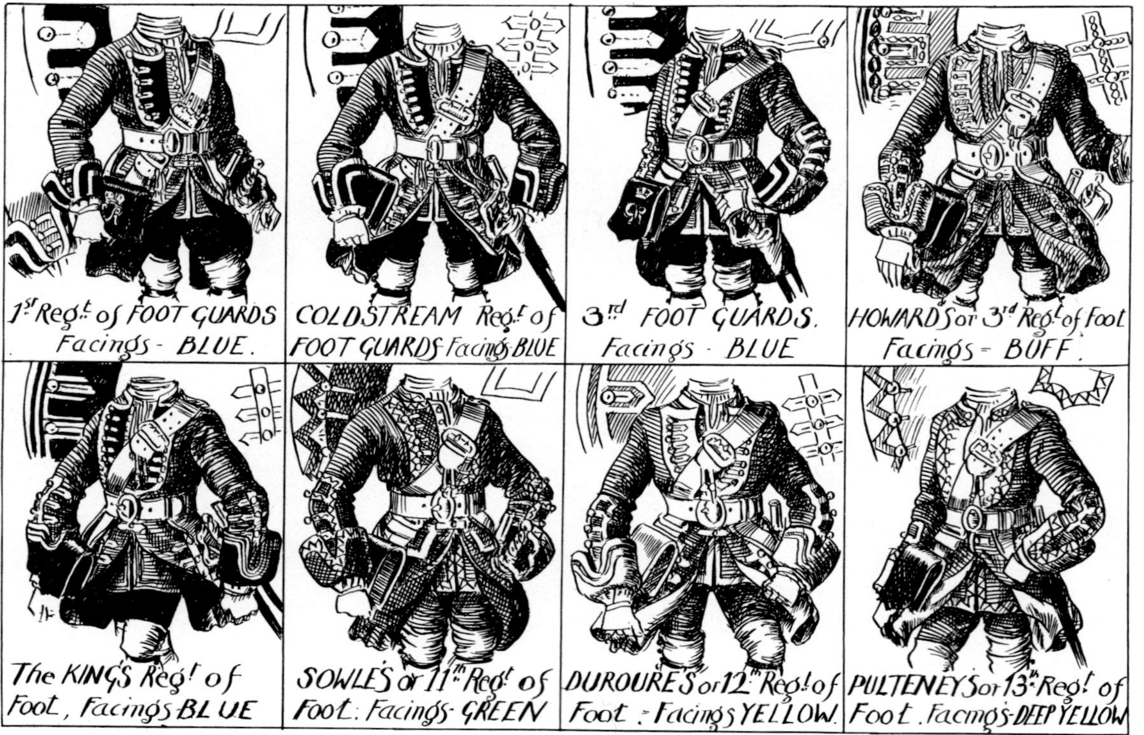

Fig.5. Uniforms of British Infantry at Dettingen, 1743

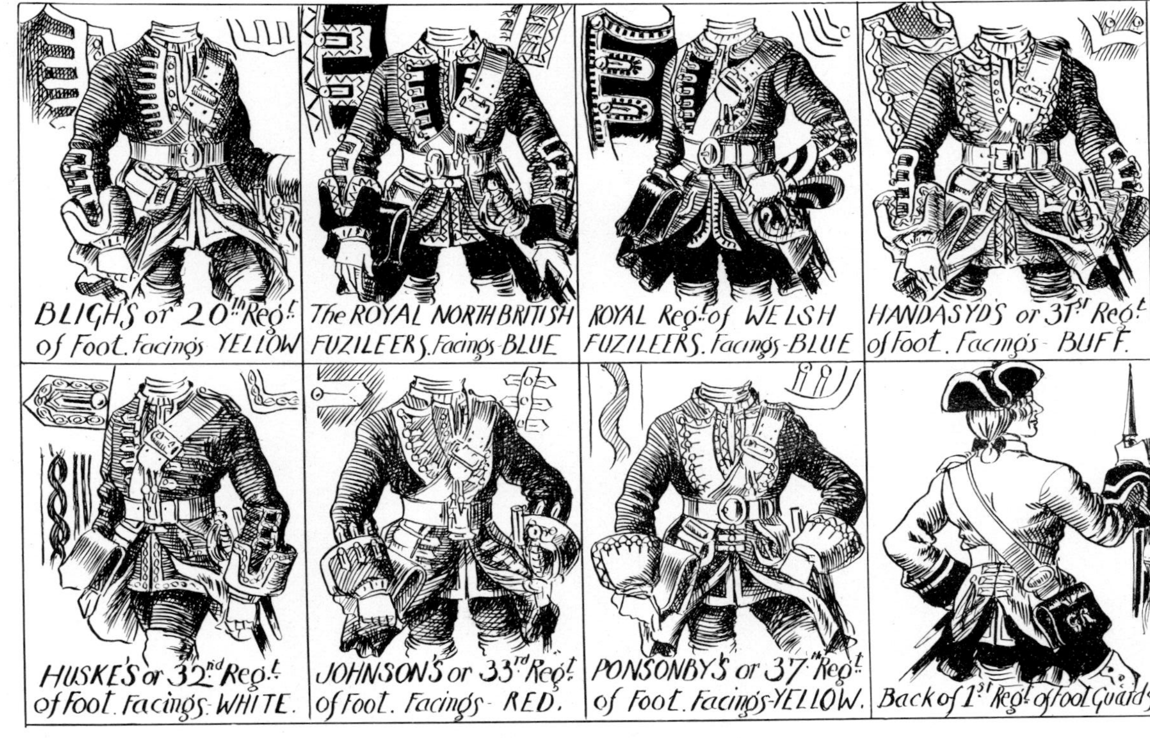

Fig.6. Uniforms of British Infantry at Dettingen, 1743

The following infantry regiments of the Austrian Army were present at Dettingen. All wore white coats, the other distinctions in dress were as follows:

Los Rios: Green facings, yellow buttons.
Arenberg: Green facings, white buttons.
D'Arberg: Red facings, yellow buttons.
de Ligne: Rose red facings, white buttons.
Salm: Black facings, white buttons.
Prié: Blue facings.
Gaisruck: Red facings.
Braunschweig-Wolfenbüttel: Blue cuffs, waistcoat and lining, yellow buttons.

In the accompanying illustration is, on the left, a grenadier of the Regiment of Los Rios. His uniform is white with green facings, linings and waistcoat, brass buttons and a black cravat. His breeches are buff and he has black gaiters. The cap-bag is green with gold lace and tassel. The sword is curved, almost oriental in pattern. Like the hussars "love-locks" were worn by grenadiers.

The colour of the facings, cap-bags, cravats and breeches varied in different regiments.

On the right is a battalion man of the Line. His uniform is white; the facings varied for different regiments. A pompom is on the hat; no sword is carried, only a bayonet.

Below is, on the left, a waist-pouch worn by some grenadiers, black with a brass grenade. In the centre a brass match-box and on the right the back of a grenadier's cap.

Fig.7. Austrian Infantry, 1743

The three regiments of Foot Guards and twelve of the Line took part in this engagement. A description of their dress is shown in the table below.

The details have been taken from *A Representation of the*

UNIFORMS WORN BY THE

REGIMENTAL TITLE	FACINGS	BREECHES
1st Regiment of Foot Guards	Blue	Blue
Coldstream Regiment of Foot Guards	Blue	Blue
3rd Regiment of Foot Guards	Blue	Blue
Maj.-Gen. Howard's Regiment of Foot	Buff	Red
The King's Regiment of Foot (Onslow's)	Blue	Blue
Col. Sowle's Regiment of Foot	Green	Red
Col. Douroure's Regiment of Foot	Yellow	Red
Brig.-Gen. Pulteney's Regiment of Foot	Deep Yellow	Red
Col. Bligh's Regiment of Foot	Pale Yellow	Red
Royal North British Regiment of Fuzileers (Maj.-Gen. John Campbell's)	Blue	Blue
Royal Regiment of Welsh Fuzileers (Col. Newsham Pier's)	Blue	Blue
Brig.-Gen. Handasyd's Regiment of Foot	Buff	Red
Brig.-Gen. Huske's Regiment of Foot	White	Red
Col. Johnson's Regiment of Foot	Red	Red
Col. Ponsonby's Regiment of Foot	Yellow	Red

Except Bligh's which were yellow, all waistcoats were red.

Cloathing of His Majesty's Household and of all the Forces upon the Establishment of Great Britain and Ireland, 1742.

Regiments at this period could be distinguished not only by the colour of their facings but also by the pattern of their lace which was different for each regiment.

BRITISH INFANTRY AT DETTINGEN

LACE	NO. IN 1751	TITLE IN 1920
Plain White	—	Grenadier Guards
Plain White	—	Coldstream Guards
Plain White	—	Scots Guards
Red worm, two buff stripes	3rd	The Buffs (East Kent Regiment)
Two blue stripes	8th	The King's (Liverpool Regiment)
Yellow and Green Pattern	11th	The Devonshire Regiment
Yellow stripe	12th	The Suffolk Regiment
Yellow zig-zag and sprig	13th	The Somerset Light Infantry
Plain White	20th	The Lancashire Fusiliers
Blue worm and yellow stripe	21st	The Royal Scots Fusiliers
Yellow Stripe, blue stripe and red cross stripe	23rd	The Royal Welch Fusiliers
Yellow zig-zag	31st	1st Bn. The East Surrey Regiment
Green stripe, red worm	32nd	1st Bn. The Duke of Cornwall's Light Infantry
Plain White	33rd	1st Bn. The Duke of Wellington's Regiment
Yellow zig-zag	37th	1st Bn. The Hampshire Regiment

A note has already been given of the composition of the British and Austrian contingents at Dettingen, the third force was provided by the Hanoverian Army and its infantry regiments who all wore red coats were:

Sommerfeldt: Dark green facings, white buttons.
Soubiron: Yellow facings and buttons.
Monroy: Black facings, yellow buttons, straw-coloured waistcoat and linings.
Zastrow: White facings, yellow buttons.
Schulenberg: Red facings, yellow buttons.
Middachten: Lemon yellow cuff, lapel, lining and waistcoat. White buttons. Red shoulder knot.
Boselager: Straw coloured facings, white buttons.
Spörcken: Straw coloured facings, yellow buttons.
Borch: Dark green facings, white buttons and shoulder cord.

The three central figures on the colour plate are, on the left, a grenadier of the Royal North British Regiment of Fuzileers, in the centre a corporal of the Highland Regiment (In 1758 the regiment was granted the "Royal" title and the facings changed from buff to blue); and on the right an officer of a Royal Regiment which wears gold lace. Being of a battalion company he carries a spontoon, grenadier company officers carried fusils. The gorget is gilt. If a regiment wore silver lace then the gorget was silver as was also the aiguilette worn on the right shoulder.

Behind is a grenadier of the Regiment of Los Rios of the Austrian Army. White uniform with green facings, buff breeches and black gaiters. Next is a cartridge bag of Foot Guards, plain black with the Royal cypher and crown. Regiments of the Line were usually buff although Fusiliers had black.

At the top are various grenadier caps. On the left that of a regiment of Foot Guards, next that of the Royal Regiment of Welsh Fuzileers. In the centre is the back of the cap of the 12th Regiment of Foot, the number in roman numerals being on either side of the grenade. The hair was tucked up underneath the cap.

British and Allied Infantry, 1743

Beside this is the front of a cap of a regiment which had yellow facings, the Royal cypher was usually in black on white although sometimes blue. The White Horse of Hanover on red with the motto "Nec aspera terrent" above.

The last illustration is that of the Regiment of Soubiron of the Hanoverian Army. The uniform of the regiment was red with yellow facings, white equipment was worn. Some grenadier caps of the Hanoverian Army had metal fronts.

THE HIGHLAND REGIMENT

The Black Watch as we know it today did not join the Allied Army until after Dettingen, but received its baptism of fire at Fontenoy.

It wore the distinctive Highland garb as shown in the accompanying illustration.

The central figure, an officer, wears a short red jacket without lapels, lined buff, a red waistcoat and flat blue bonnet. His belted plaid is of the regimental sett of dark blue, black and green and white; cloth hose striped red.

His sporran is made of either otter, doe, seal or deer-skin, with the hair outside, usually a metal clasp-top, often ornamented and leather thongs knotted at end to form tassels.

A crimson sash is worn over the left shoulder and he is armed with a fusil, a broad sword, a dirk on the right side and a claw-butted Highland pistol with iron or brass stock carried on a narrow pistol-belt.

On the left is a piper. His uniform is red with light buff facings and a blue bonnet. The pipes had three drones and the bag was of a plain colour. It was not changed to tartan until late in the 18th century. The pipe banner is a red cross on a yellow field.

On the right is a sergeant who also has a red coat with buff cuffs and a red waistcoat, and blue bonnet. Besides the halberd he is carrying he is armed with sword, dirk and pistol carried on a narrow pistol-belt.

In the background are two Highlanders wearing the belted plaid. This was in fact the plaid and kilt in one and was made up of 12 yards double width of tartan. Belted round the centre the

Fig.8. The Highland Regiment, 1745

lower half formed the kilt and the upper half the plaid and by loosening the belt the whole became a blanket or plaid. Plaid being the Gaelic word for blanket.

Above are some of the accoutrements in greater detail; left to right: a cartridge pouch of black leather inscribed G.R. and crown; a broad-sword hilt, the length of the sword overall was 39½″, the blade 33¼″; a dirk, length overall 20¾″, blade 16½″; a claw-butted pistol with iron or brass stock.

Targets (circular shields) were permitted and were furnished by the Colonel or the men themselves. These targets were studded with nails and were sometimes furnished with a spike in the central boss.

LORD CHARLES HAY AT FONTENOY

The British advanced, as Fortescue in his *History* says "Forward tramped the ranks of scarlet, silent and stately as if on parade". When they had advanced to within fifty yards of the French, Lord Charles Hay of the First Guards stepped forward with flask in hand and doffing his hat drank politely to his enemies. "I hope, gentlemen," he shouted, "that you are going to wait for us today and not swim the Scheldt as you swam the Main at Dettingen, men of the King's Company", he continued, turning round to his own people, "these are the French Guards, and I hope you are going to beat them today"; and the English Guards answered with a cheer.

The illustration shows the salute with the spontoon, the spontoon being held in the right hand horizontally on the shoulder, while the left hand carried the hat. Note also the size of the Colours, at this period they were 6ft. 6ins. by 6ft. 2ins.

The artist is indebted to Charles Stadden for his article on the Gardes Françaises, 1745-50 in *Tradition* Vol iv. No.24.

Fig.9. Lord Charles Hay at Fontenoy

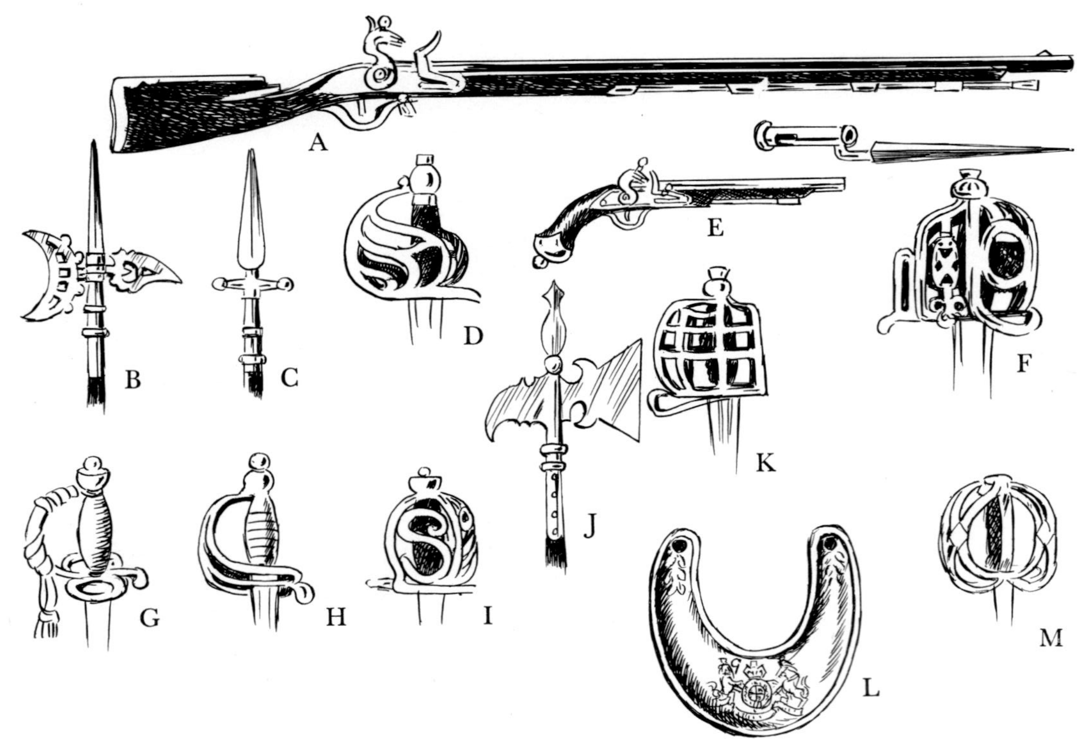

Fig.10 Arms of the British Soldier

ARMS OF THE BRITISH SOLDIER, 1743-60

A "Brown Bess" musket and bayonet.
The musket had a barrel of 46 inches and fired bullets 14 to the pound. The ramrod was made of wood with a brass top. Rate of fire was two or three rounds a minute.
B and J Two types of sergeants' halberds. Chiefly used for dressing the line.
C Officers' spontoon. In 1743 all officers of battalion companies carried spontoons. This weapon was abolished in 1786.
D and M Dragoons' sword. Had a straight blade of 31 inches.
E Cavalry pistol.
F Cavalry sword: The oval ring enabled the rider to shorten his reins without letting go of his sword.
G An infantry officer's sword.
H A battalion man's sword. When discontinued by battalion companies it was retained by grenadier companies.
I A grenadier's basket-hilted sword.
K Sword as carried by Horse Guards.
L Officer's gorget. Worn when officer was on duty. Abolished in 1830.

The swords differed from regiment to regiment; some being straight, others curved, according to the wishes of the Colonel. The length of the blade varied from 30 to 35 inches.

Information on these weapons has been culled from the following works. where fuller details may be found.

A History of the Uniforms of the British Army. Cecil C. P. Lawson.
Sword, Lance and Bayonet. Charles ffoulkes.
British Military Fire-Arms. Blackmore.
Weapons of the British Soldier. Colonel H. C. B. Rogers.
Scottish Swords and Dirks. John Wallace.

THE FRENCH CAVALRY, 1743-45

Both the Maison du Roi and the Cavalry of the Line were represented at Dettingen and the uniforms worn were:

Maison du Roi.

Garde du Corps:
Compagnie Ecossaise: Blue coat, red lining and waistcoat, silver lace, red breeches and stockings, silver shoulder-belts with white silk squares in the centre. Red shabraque, edged silver.
Compagnie Première Française: As above but green squares on the belt and green shabraque.
Compagnie Seconde Française: As above but blue squares on the belt and blue shabraque.
Compagnie Troisième Française: As above but yellow squares on the belt and yellow shabraque.
Première Compagnie des Mousquetaires (Gris): Scarlet coat, lining and cuffs; scarlet waistcoat; gold lace and gilt buttons, vertical pockets, red breeches and stockings, gold hat lace. Blue supervest lined red and edged with silver lace; on front and back a white cross with red and silver flames. Red shabraque edged with gold lace.
Seconde Compagnie des Mousquetaires (Noirs): As above but with silver instead of gold lace. On the supervest the flames are yellow and silver.
Compagnie des Gensdarmes de la Garde: Scarlet coat, red lining, black velvet cuff, cross pockets, gold lace and embroidery, gilt buttons. Chamois waistcoat laced and edged with gold lace. Red breeches and stockings, gold hat lace and white plume. Red shabraque edged with gold lace.
Other companies of Gensdarmes had the same uniform as above but the facings varied. Gensdarmes de la Reine had red facings; Dauphin: sky-blue; Anjou: green; Orleans: blue.
Compagnie des Chevaux-Legers de la Garde: Scarlet coat, red lining, black velvet cuff, cross pockets, gold lace with silver laced button-holes and buttons. Chamois waistcoat laced with gold and with silver buttons. Breeches and stockings red, silver hat lace, white plume. Scarlet shabraque edged silver.

Colonel General: Red coat and lining, black plush lapel and cuff, yellow buttons, leather breeches, white belts, gold hat lace, red shabraque edged with black and white lace.

Royal: Blue coat, red lapels, cuffs and linings. Yellow buttons, white belts, leather breeches, gold hat lace. Blue shabraque with a border.

La Reine: Red coat, royal blue lining and cuffs, yellow buttons, yellow belts edged with white, gold hat lace. Red shabraque edged with lace of the Queen's livery; yellow fleurs-de-lis on front and back parts.

Royal Pologne: Blue coat, red lining, collar and cuff; blue and white aiguillette, white buttons, yellow belts, leather breeches, silver hat lace. Blue shabraque with blue and white edge.

Carabiniers: Blue coat and collar, red cuff and lining. White buttons three and three on the coat. Epaulettes and cuffs edged with silver lace, buff waistcoat, leather breeches, silver hat lace. Blue shabraque edged with silver lace.

Condé: Grey-white coat, red cuff and lining, grey cloth buttons in pairs. White belts, leather breeches, silver hat lace. Fawn coloured shabraque with the Condé arms embroidered in silk and a crimson lace edge.

Conty: Cinder-grey coat, lining, cuff and buttons. Buff belts, golden yellow aiguillette, leather breeches, gold hat lace. Fawn coloured shabraque with the Prince's coat-of-arms on the corner.

Orleans: Grey-white coat, red lapels, cuff and lining. Grey cloth buttons, yellow belts, leather breeches, silver hat lace. Red shabraque edged with white.

D'Heudicourt: Grey-white coat, red lapels, cuff and lining. Fawn waistcoat and breeches, yellow buttons, gold hat lace. Red shabraque edged white.

Pentièvre: Grey-white coat, red cuff and lining, yellow buttons, white belts, leather breeches, gold hat lace, red shabraque.

Royal Dragoons: Blue coat, red lining, cuffs, breeches and waistcoat, white button-holes three and three. The waistcoat had a white edge, white buttons. Blue bonnet turned up with red and lined white. Leather breeches, white stockings, silver hat lace. Blue shabraque edged white.

French Cavalry, 1743-45

Bercheny Hussars: Bright blue dolman and pelisse, red lining. White buttons and lace, blue breeches, red cap trimmed with bearskin. Red shabraque with golden yellow fleurs-de-lis, white border.

Du Roi Cavalry: Blue coat, red lining and cuffs, yellow buttons, white belts, leather breeches, gold hat lace. Blue shabraque edged golden yellow.

Du Roi Dragoons: Blue coat and lining, red cuffs, waistcoat and breeches. White buttons and lace loops on coat and cuff. Golden yellow shoulder strap. Blue cap. Blue shabraque edged golden yellow.

The colour plate depicts mounted a Gendarme of the Garde du Corps Maison du Roi, and a Gendarme de la Garde Ordinaire du Roi. He has black facings. Dismounted are a Grenadier à cheval, with, in the centre the Seconde Compagnie des Mousquetaires (Noirs) Maison du Roi. His lace is silver and he rode a black horse. The Première Compagnie (Gris) had gold lace and rode grey horses. On the right is the Cuirassiers du Roi.

FRENCH INFANTRY, 1743-45

The French Infantry that fought at Dettingen were dressed as follows:

Maison du Roi Infantry.

Gardes Françaises: Blue coat, red lining, cuff and waistcoat. White lace loops in threes on the front of the coat, white buttons, the waistcoat edged with white. Chamois belts edged with white. Red ammunition pouch with the Royal Arms, the pouch edged golden yellow. Red breeches and stockings. Silver hat lace.

Line Infantry.

All wore grey-white coats, other details were:

Navarre: All grey-white uniform, yellow buttons, shield-shaped pocket with nine buttons, gold hat lace.

Bigorre: Blue cuffs, yellow buttons and hat lace.

Le Roi: Blue lining, cuff, waistcoat, breeches and stockings, yellow buttons, golden yellow lace loops in threes on the coat and waistcoat down to the pockets. Gold hat lace.

Orleans: Red cuff, yellow buttons, four on sleeve and four on pocket. Gold hat lace.

Royal la Marine: Blue cuff, white buttons. Silver hat lace.

Vexin: Blue cuff, yellow buttons. Gold hat lace.

Auvergne: Red cuff, white buttons. Silver hat lace.

Artois: All grey-white uniform. Yellow buttons. Gold hat lace.

Condé: Red cuff, yellow buttons. Gold hat lace.

Touraine: Blue cuff, white buttons, vertical pockets, silver hat lace.

Chartres: Red cuff, yellow buttons. Gold hat lace.

Rohan: Red cuffs, white buttons. Silver hat lace.

Dauphin: Blue cuff, vertical pockets, yellow buttons. Gold hat lace.

Aubeterre: Red cuff, white buttons. Silver hat lace.

D'Eu: Blue collar and cuff, yellow buttons four on cuff and three on cross pocket. Gold hat lace.

Mortemart: Red cuff, yellow buttons alternating with white ones. Gold and Silver hat lace.

La Marche: Red cuff, yellow buttons. Gold hat lace.

Pentièvre: Royal blue cuff, white buttons. Silver hat lace.

Hainault: Red cuff, yellow buttons. Gold hat lace.

Piémont: Black cuffs, yellow buttons. Gold hat lace.

The colour plate shows a soldier of a Royal regiment and therefore has blue facings. Facing him is an officer and men of the Gardes Françaises, they have blue uniforms with red facings. The Gardes Suisses had red uniforms with blue facings as did the Irish troops in the French service.

French Infantry, 1743-45

DRAGOONS MARCHING ORDER, 1751

The illustration shows the appearance of a dragoon in marching order. He is of the 7th or Queen's Own Dragoons. His uniform is red with white facings, breeches scarlet, loops white and white metal buttons. The hat lace is silver. Shabraque and holster caps white, lace yellow with blue stripe. The Queen's cypher on the holster-caps is yellow.

Fig.11. Marching Order, 7th or Queen's Own Dragoons, 1751

A White shoulder knot.
C Breastplate to stop saddle slipping backwards.
E Carbine bucket.
G Cloak.
J Crupper and docked tail.
L Bit and bridoon.
N Pistol (barrel 12″ long).

B Flounces and strap to support carbine.
D Pistol.
F Buff cartridge pouch.
H Shabraque.
K Cavalry sword with various sword-hilts.
M Stirrup irons.

Other items not shown in the illustration and which were carried are a round brown water-bottle, a canvas feed-bag and a haversack. Tent or picket-poles if carried were probably strapped to the carbine with the end in the carbine bucket.

All this impedimenta would be discarded when the cavalry were in action to be retrieved when the engagement was over.

FARRIERS.

The illustration is based on a painting by David Morier of a farrier of the 11th Dragoons.

The uniform is as follows: Dark blue coat with red patches on the collar, and red cuffs. White braid loops in threes, pale buff lining, pale buff waistcoat and breeches with white cotton knee-pieces above the boots; greyish apron tucked up round the waist, black leather pouch hung over the left shoulder by a narrow buff strap, buff gauntlet gloves; black bearskin cap with red cloth bag, and front of red enamel bordered with white metal, bearing a white metal device of a horse-shoe with pincers and hammer on either side, pale buff housing, bordered with white mohair lace with a green stripe in the centre; device XI D in white on a red ground, within a wreath of roses and thistles; no holster caps, but instead a black leather churn in front, with dark grey or black fur covering; red cloak rolled with the pale buff lining outside, at rear; all reins etc. of black leather, the horse is one of the dark browns on which the regiment was mounted for many years.

When the regiment was ordered to "draw swords" the farriers "ported axes" as in the drawing. The churn contained horse-shoes, nails, hammers and pincers.

Fig.12. Farrier, 11th Dragoons, 1751

LIGHT TROOPS.

At the end of 1755 a troop of light dragoons (sixty-five men) was added to each of the eleven regiments of dragoons on the British establishment. They were mounted on light horses of the hunter class of shades of bay and brown. Their accoutrements were extremely light, they carried short carbines with ring and bar 4′ 3″ long, with a 17″ bayonet, a pistol 10″ long including the barrel and of carbine bore and a straight cutting sword 34″ with a light hilt without basket.

Fig.13. Private, Light Troop, 11th Dragoons

These Light Troops were disbanded in 1763 but complete regiments of Light Dragoons were now being raised commencing with the 15th Light Dragoons in 1759.

Fig.13 is based on a painting by David Morier. The cap is black with a red front with "G.R." crowned and some embroidery round the edge all shown in yellow. It has a small white plume. The coat is red with white lace and deep yellow turnbacks. The waistcoat and breeches are the same deep yellow with white metal buttons. The pouch and belt are of brown leather. The sword has a brass hilt. The holster caps and housings are yellow edged with white, green, white. A black leather pistol holster shows below the cap, the design is obscured by a white hair top, it had a large "G.R." on it. In the point of the housing are "XI D" on red cloth with a green wreath. There is a rolled red cloak behind the saddle. The private is riding on a loose bit rein.

BRITISH CAVALRY IN THE SEVEN YEARS' WAR

Fourteen regiments of British cavalry participated in the war, and details of their dress is shown in the table on pages 40 and 41.

The colour plate shows the mounted figures of a private of the Royal Horse Guards and a trooper of the Luckner Hussars of the Hanoverian Army. Dismounted are an officer of the Royal Artillery and privates of the Light Troop, 11th Dragoons, a regiment of Horse of the Hanoverian Army and the 1st King's Dragoon Guards.

The powder flask of the Blues is carried by a flask cord, an item of dress which is still worn by the Household Cavalry today. The officer of the Royal Artillery is carrying a fusil and the private of the Light Troop is wearing the distinctive headdress which was worn by these troops.

The private of the Hanoverian Horse is wearing the field mark of a sprig of oak in his hat. The King's Dragoon Guards were formerly ranked as the 2nd Regiment of Horse, but with the 3rd and 4th Horse became the 1st, 2nd and 3rd Dragoon Guards in 1746, the remaining regiments of Horse were converted to Dragoon Guards in 1788.

British and Allied Cavalry, 1759-60

REGIMENT	COLOUR OF FACINGS AND LAPELS	BUTTONS	WAISTCOAT BREECHES LINING OF COAT AND CLOAKS	HAT LACE
Royal Horse Guards, Blue	Red	Yellow	Red	Gold
1st (King's) Dragoon Guards	Blue with Half Lapels	Yellow	Blue	Gold
2nd The Queen's Dragoon Guards	Buff with Half Lapels	Yellow	Buff	Gold
3rd Regiment of Dragoon Guards	White with Half Lapels	Yellow	White	Gold
2nd Irish Horse	Full Green Lapelled	Yellow	Full Green	Gold
3rd Regiment of Horse or the Carabineers	Pale Yellow Lapelled	White	Pale Yellow	Silver
4th Irish Horse	Black Lapelled	Yellow	Buff	Gold
1st (Royal) Dragoons	Blue without Lapels	Yellow	Blue	Gold
2nd Royal North British Dragoons	Blue without Lapels	White	Blue	None
6th (Inniskilling) Dragoons	Full Yellow No Lapels	White	Full Yellow	Silver
7th or Queen's Own Dragoons	White No Lapels	White	White	Silver
10th Dragoons	Deep Yellow No Lapels	White	Deep Yellow	Silver
11th Dragoons	Buff No Lapels	White	Buff	Silver
15th Light Dragoons	Dark Green Lapelled	White	White	None

IN THE SEVEN YEARS' WAR

HOUSINGS AND HOLSTER CAPS

COLOUR	LACE	BADGE	TITLE IN 1920
Red	Royal	King's Cypher within Garter and Crown	Royal Horse Guards (The Blues)
Red	Royal	King's Cypher within Garter and Crown	1st King's Dragoon Guards
Buff	Royal	Queen's Cypher within the Garter	The Queen's Bays (2nd Dragoon Guards)
White	Yellow and Red Stripe	Rank of the Regiment III D.G.	3rd Dragoon Guards (Prince of Wales's)
Full Green	White and Red Stripe	Rank of the Regiment II H.	5th Dragoon Guards (Princess Charlotte of Wales's)
Pale Yellow	White and Red Stripe	Rank of the Regiment III H.	Carabiniers (6th Dragoon Guards)
Buff	White and Black Stripe	Rank of the Regiment IV H.	7th Dragoon Guards (Princess Royal's)
Red	Royal	Crest of England within The Garter	1st The Royal Dragoons
Blue	Royal	Thistle within the circle of St. Andrew	The Royal Scots Greys (2nd Dragoons)
Full Yellow	White and Blue Stripe	Castle of Inniskilling within a Wreath	The Inniskillings (6th Dragoons)
White	Royal	Queen's Cypher within the Garter	7th Queen's Own Hussars
Deep Yellow	White and Green Stripe	Rank of the Regiment X.D.	10th Royal Hussars (Prince of Wales's Own)
Buff	White and Green Stripe	Rank of the Regiment XI.D.	11th Hussars (Prince Albert's Own)

Green saddle cloth laced white with a red stripe. King's Cypher and Crown on forepart and L.D. within a Wreath on the back part.	15th (The King's) Hussars

ARTILLERY IN THE SEVEN YEARS' WAR

During the Seven Years' War the English guns were noted for being kept the cleanest and in the best order of all the artillery in Ferdinand's army.

The lighter pieces such as 3-pdrs and 6-pdrs were still attached to infantry, but were served by gunners of the artillery. Two guns were allowed to a battalion and the detachment consisted of an officer, 2 N.C.O.s and twelve men.

At Minden the guns consisted of medium 12 pounders which were fired on the French cavalry at a range of 900 to 1,000 yards. Usually five horses were harnessed to a gun, but at Minden a team consisted of seven. These were probably in pairs, except the wheeler in single harness in the shafts.

ROSES AT MINDEN

It is a tradition that the British infantry in their advance plucked roses and put them in their hats. This cannot be substantiated but for many years the regiments (with the exception of the Royal Welch Fusiliers) that fought at Minden have celebrated the anniversary with the wearing of roses. The Lancashire Fusiliers decorated their drums and drum-major's staff with red and yellow roses and the Colours bore a wreath of the same colours, whilst all ranks wore a red rose on the right and a yellow on the left of their headdress.

The King's Own Yorkshire Light Infantry wore a white rose on the side of the cap and the drum-major's staff was also decorated.

The King's Own Scottish Borderers, the Suffolk Regiment and the Royal Hampshire Regiment wore red roses in the headdress, but did not decorate their drums or Colours.

Roses are also worn by two Royal Artillery batteries which are the descendants of those that fought at Minden.

A Rose for Minden

"You got a rose, Jim, same as me,
Wearin' 'n all down the line, they be,
Folks in Lyndhurst would call us scats
Fightin' wiv roses in our 'ats."

J. S. HICKS

(Reproduced by permission of *Punch*.)

REGIMENT	FACINGS	WAISTCOAT	BREECHES
12th Foot (Napier's)	Yellow	Red	Red
20th Foot (Kingsley's)	Pale Yellow	Red	Red
23rd Foot (Huske's) (Prince of Wales's Own Royal Regiment of Welsh Fuzileers)	Blue	Red	Blue
25th Foot (Home's)	Deep Yellow	Red	Red
37th Foot (Stewart's)	Yellow	Red with lace across	Red
51st Foot (Brudenell's)	Green	Red	Red

BRITISH INFANTRY IN THE SEVEN YEARS' WAR

The first contingent of six regiments of Foot fought at Minden, these were reinforced in 1760 by a second contingent consisting of the 2nd battalions of the three Regiments of Foot Guards, and the 5th, 8th, 11th, 24th, 33rd and 50th Foot, as well as the 88th Highlanders (Campbells') who were disbanded in 1763 on the conclusion of the war.

The main dress distinctions of these additional regiments were:

BRITISH REGIMENTS AT MINDEN

LACE	OFFICERS' LACE	TITLE IN 1920
White with yellow stripe	Gold (white for Other Ranks' Hats)	The Suffolk Regiment
White with two black and two red stripes	Silver	The Lancashire Fusiliers
White with yellow and black stripe	Gold	The Royal Welch Fusiliers
White with blue and red zig-zag	Gold	The King's Own Scottish Borderers
White with red and blue zig-zag and two yellow stripes between	Silver	The Hampshire Regiment
White with green worm	Gold	The King's Own Yorkshire Light Infantry

5th Foot: Facings and linings green, white and green lace.
8th Foot: Facings and linings blue, white and yellow lace.
11th Foot: Facings and linings green, white and green lace.
24th Foot: Facings willow green, white linings, white and green lace.
33rd Foot: Facings red, white linings, plain lace.
50th Foot: Facings black, white and red lace.

British and Allied Infantry, 1759-60

46

In the top left hand corner of the colour plate is the head of an officer's espontoon as carried in the Hanoverian Army, and the two top figures are those of Allies. On the left a grenadier of the Hesse-Cassel Foot Guards and on the right a private of a Hanoverian Regiment of the Infantry of the Line which had yellow facings.

Below is a private of a battalion company of the 20th Foot and two figures showing the front and back of grenadiers in marching order of the 12th Foot.

The Hanoverian Army dress was very similar to the British Infantry except that they wore tassels and a rosette in their hats and wore black cravats. The men too were allowed to wear moustaches.

In marching order grenadiers wore the coat done up and carried a cowhide knapsack, a white metal water-bottle and grey canvas haversack. Grenadiers still carried curved swords, they were done away with in 1762. The battalion companies carried straight swords until these were abolished in 1745. Belts were of buff leather and pouches black.

Other distinctions at this period were corporals had a white worsted loop on the right shoulder, whereas sergeants had a crimson and white waist-sash and carried swords and halberds.

DRUMMERS AND FIFERS

The Royal Warrant of 1751 gave details of the dress of drummers and fifers. The coats for all Royal regiments to be red faced and lapelled with blue and laced with Royal lace. The waistcoat, breeches and the lining of the coats to be of the same colour as that which is ordered for their respective regiments. Coats of regiments which are faced with red to be white, faced, lapelled and lined in red, red waistcoats and breeches. All other regiments to be of the colour of the facings of the regiment faced and lapelled with red. The waistcoats of those which have buff or white coats to be red, all others the same as the men.

The drummers' cap was similar to the grenadier but instead of being stiffened, hung down at the back in the form of a bag with a tassel. The front was of facings colour embroidered with trophies of drums and Colours.

Fig. 15. Fifer, 1745 (after Hogarth), Drummer of a Royal regiment, 1751 (after Morier), Drummers' cap, 1751, Fife case, 1745

In the illustration the white horse is on a blue little flap on the fifer but on red on the 1751 cap, the hanging sleeves are blue inside. The drummer's lace is blue with yellow spots and edging. Both figures have red coats and waistcoats and blue breeches, lace blue edged yellow. The drums are blue with red rims and are emblazoned with the Royal Arms. The cord on the fife case is red and white. Note the drummer is carrying a water-bottle.

THE MARQUIS OF GRANBY

The Marquis of Granby (1721-1770) became Colonel of The Blues in 1755. He succeeded Lord George Sackville as commander-in-chief of the British troops in Germany.

His kindness of heart made him very popular with the British Army, and he did all in his power to relieve the distress of the soldiers during the privations of the campaign.

Being so popular it is not surprising that so many inns in the country were named "The Marquis of Granby" as this no doubt attracted the custom of those who had served under him.

He led the British cavalry at the Battle of Warburg, 31st July, 1760. During the advance he lost both hat and wig and his bald head shining in the sun gave rise to the expression "Going for it bald-headed".

Fig.16. "Going for it bald-headed"

The British cavalry were ordered by Ferdinand to ride on ahead of the infantry, they had five miles to cover but trotting and cantering most of the way they caught the French cavalry in the act of preparing to retire and both cavalry and infantry were put in full flight.

The cavalry that took part in this action were 14 squadrons in the first line consisting of 1st King's Dragoon Guards, 3rd Dragoon Guards, 2nd Dragoon Guards, The Blues, 7th Dragoon Guards and The Carabiniers. In the second line were eight squadrons of The Greys, 10th Dragoons, Inniskillings and 11th Dragoons.

Fig.17. A Camp Scene

A sutleress offers for sale a duck which she has probably purloined from a neighbouring farm.

Sutlers were officially recognised, one being allowed per Troop of Cavalry or Company of Foot. They received an allowance of forage from the commissaries for their horses.

All extra provisions and liquor were supplied by the sutlers who played an important part in the well-being of the Army.

Sutleresses sometimes dressed in soldiers' discarded clothing. The one in the illustration based on Morier's picture is wearing a bright green jacket, red waistcoat with white lace loops, brown skirt, light blue apron, blue stockings and red rosettes on her shoes.

Tents of the ridge-pole type held six men. Bell tents or bells of arms as they were termed were used for storing arms in the field.

THE GERMAN CONTINGENTS IN THE ALLIED ARMY

The German contingents in the Allied Army were provided by Hanover and Prussia fighting as allies; and by Hesse-Cassel, Brunswick, Bückeburg and Saxe Gotha fighting as mercenaries. The dress of some of these units follows:

Cavalry.
Hanoverian.

Horse Grenadiers: Red coat and lining, black lapel and cuff, straw-coloured waistcoats, gold lace, grenadier cap with black front.

Breitenbach: White coat, no lapel, yellow cuff and lining. Three white buttons on cuff, six on coat.

Garde du Corps: Red coat, no lapel, silver lace loops, red cuffs, blue lining, straw-coloured waistcoat and breeches.

Bremer: White coat, bright green cuff and lining, silver buttons.

Veltheim: White coat, red cuff, lapel and lining, silver buttons.

Hammerstein: White coat, dark green cuff and lining, gold buttons, three on cuff.

Luckner Hussars: Black fur cap, red bag, white dolman, yellow lace, red pelisse, yellow lace, black fur. White breeches, yellow boots, red sabretache and shabraque both with White Horse and with yellow edges.

Mounted Jaegers: Cocked hat, green plume, green coat and waistcoat, white buttons, pale buff breeches, black boots, green saddle-cloth, pale buff shoulder-belt.

Hessian

Prinz Wilhelm: Straw-coloured coat, blue collar and cuff, blue waistcoat, gold lace.

Lieb Regiment: Straw-coloured coat, red collar and cuff, blue waistcoat, gold lace.

Pruschenk: Straw-coloured coat, bright blue cuff, collar and waistcoat, silver lace.

Miltiz: Straw-coloured coat with green facings.

Infantry.

Hanoverian.

Foot Guards: Red coat, dark blue lapel, cuff and lining, blue waistcoat, yellow lace and buttons.

Hardenburg: Red coat, orange cuff, lining and waistcoat, white buttons.

Rheden: Red coat, white cuff, lapel and lining, white buttons.

Scheele: Red coat, straw-coloured cuff, lapel and lining, yellow buttons.

Stolzemberg: Red coat, black cuff and lapel, straw-coloured lining and waistcoat, white buttons.

Brunck: Red coat, medium green cuff, lapel and lining, white buttons.

Kielmannsegge: Red coat, sea-green facings, white lining, waistcoat and buttons.

Hesse-Cassel.

Erbprinz von Hessen: Blue coat, yellow lapel and collar, white buttons.

Hessian Garde Regiment: Blue coat, red lapel, white lace.

Toll: Blue coat, orange lapel, yellow buttons.

Prinz von Anhalt: Blue coat, red lapel and collar, white buttons.

Bischhausen: Blue coat, yellow lapel, white lace, yellow buttons.

Mannsbach: Blue coat, white lapel, yellow buttons.

Prinz Wilhelm (Hanau): Blue coat, crimson lapel, white buttons.

Gilsac: Blue coat, red lapel, yellow buttons.

Hessian Grenadiers: Blue coat, red cuff, straw-coloured waistcoat, gold buttons.

Lieb: Blue coat, yellow lace and buttons.

Brunswick.

Imhoff: Blue coat, white waistcoat, lace and buttons.

THE LIEB GARDE OF HANOVER

The Lieb Garde or Household Troops consisted of the Garde du Corps and the Horse Grenadiers.

The Garde du Corps wore red coats without lapels, and with three pairs of silver lace button-holes, cuffs and turnbacks blue; blue collar edged silver, lace silver; pocket flaps edged silver, hat lace silver; breeches and waistcoat straw-colour. Shoulder belt buff with central stripe of blue, outer edge laced silver. Cloak blue, Housings and holster caps red edged silver, device of G.R. within the Garter surmounted by a crown worked in silver. The regiment was mounted on grey horses.

The Horse Grenadiers had red coats with red turnbacks, black lapels and cuffs edged gold, gold loops on lapels and cuffs. On the right shoulder a red shoulder-knot. A red cloth cap with black velvet front embroidered with the Royal Arms and supporters. The little flap red edged gold and with the White Horse of Hanover. Tuft red and gold. Breeches and waistcoat straw-colour.

Horse furniture red, zig-zag lace of gold with a black centre and another on the outer edge of gold with a black diamond pattern. On housings and holster caps the Royal cypher G.R. and crown in gold. Cloak red.

Equipment buff. Girth red and white. Sword hilt brass with a shell design. The regiment was mounted on black or dark brown horses.

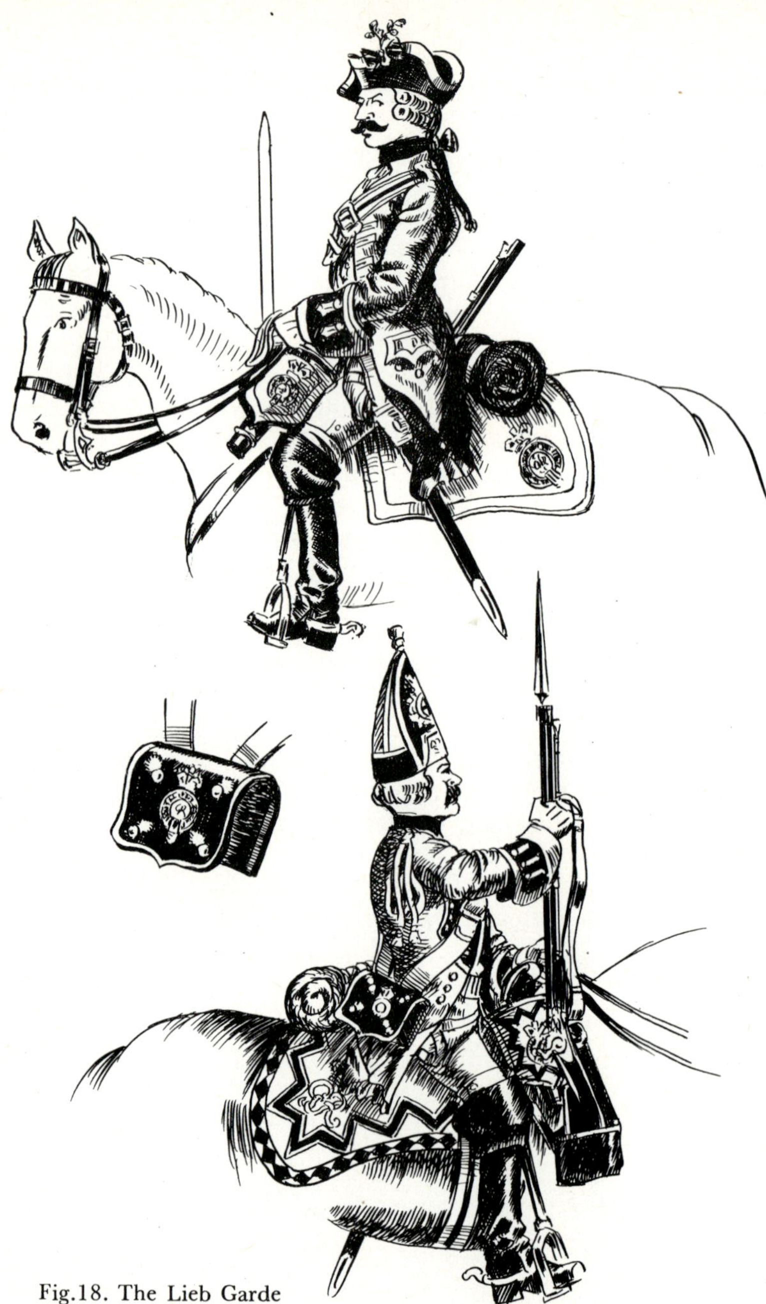

Fig.18. The Lieb Garde
Top: Garde du Corps (wearing the field sign of a sprig of oak leaves in
his headdress).   Bottom: Horse Grenadiers.
Pouch of Horse Grenadiers and Dragoons.

THE FRENCH CAVALRY AT MINDEN

In 1759 five of the 63 cavalry regiments and 12 of the 16 of dragoons wore red coats. Regiments led by Princes of the Blood wore blue. Some regiments of the Maison du Roi wore red, but the Gardes Françaises wore blue and the Gardes Suisses red, however the vast majority wore coats of greyish-white, with waistcoats and breeches a light buff. The cocked hat was worn by all units.

Fitzjames: A red uniform with dark blue lapels and lining. White hat lace and buttons; red saddle cloth.

Colonel General: A red uniform and lining, black cuff and lapel. Yellow hat lace and buttons. Red saddle cloth edged with white lace with a pattern of black squares.

Marçieux: Red lapel, cuff and lining. White lace and buttons. Green saddle cloth edged white.

Vogue: White lapel, red cuff and lining. White hat lace and buttons. Red saddle cloth, edged red.

Condé: All details greyish-white. White hat lace and buttons. Fawn saddle cloth edged red.

Cravattes: Dark blue coat with red cuff and lining. White lace loops on blue lapel. White hat lace and buttons. Blue saddle cloth.

Taleirand: White-grey lapel, red cuff and lining. White hat lace and buttons. Red saddle cloth, edged red.

Surgère: All red uniform including waistcoat and breeches. There were white lace loops down the front of the coat to the waist and three vertical loops above the cuffs. Red cap edged white. Red saddle cloth, edged white.

Poly: Red lapel, cuff, lining and breeches. White hat lace and buttons. Yellow saddle cloth, edged yellow.

D'Espinal: Red lapel, cuff and lining. Yellow hat lace, white buttons. Red saddle cloth, edged red.

Fumel: Red lapel, cuff and lining. Mixed red, white, yellow and black aiguillette. White hat lace and buttons. Red saddle cloth, edged red.

Du Roi: Blue coat and lapel, red cuff and lining. Yellow hat lace and buttons. Blue saddle cloth with a red and white patterned edge.

Enrichemont: Red lapel and cuff, white lining. White hat lace, yellow buttons. Red saddle cloth, edged red.

Moustier: Red lapel, cuff and lining. White hat lace and buttons. Red saddle cloth, edged red.

Noé: White lapel, red cuff and lining. White lace and buttons. Red saddle cloth, edged red.

Bourgogne: Blue coat, red cuff and lining. White hat lace and buttons. Blue saddle cloth, edged white.

Rougrave (also known as Volontaires Liègeois): Blue coat, yellow collar, cuff, shoulder strap and lining. White lace loops on lapel in pairs, two loops on cuff and loops on yellow waistcoat. Fur cap with blue bag. White breeches. Blue saddle cloth, edged white.

Archaic: Red lapel, white-grey cuff and lining. White hat lace and buttons. Red saddle cloth, edged red.

Royal Etranger: Blue coat, red lapel, cuff and lining. White hat lace and buttons. Blue saddle cloth.

Noailles: All details red. Yellow hat lace and buttons.

Gendarmerie de France: Uniform scarlet, laced silver. The shoulder-belts were of different colours according to companies.

Crussol: Red cuff and lining, grey-white lapel. White hat lace and yellow buttons. Red saddle cloth, edged red.

Carabiniers: Blue coat, shoulder strap piped white all round. Red cuff and lining. White piping round the top of the cuff. White hat lace and buttons. Blue saddle cloth, edged white.

Commissaire-General: Black lapel and cuff, grey-white lining. Yellow hat lace and buttons. Red saddle cloth, edged red.

Lameth: Red lapel, cuff and lining. White hat lace, yellow buttons. Red saddle cloth, edged red.

Pentièvre: Grey-white lapel, red cuff and lining. Yellow hat lace and buttons. Red saddle cloth with white edge and red squares down the middle.

Toussaint: Red lapel and cuff, grey lining. White hat lace and buttons. Red saddle cloth, edged green.

Royal Allemand: Blue, no lapel, coat edged with white piping. Red cuff, lining and waistcoat. Three white loops on cuffs. Fur cap with red bag. White buttons. Blue saddle cloth, edged white.

Wurttemburg: Red lapel, cuff and lining. White hat lace and buttons. Yellow saddle cloth, edged black.

French Cavalry, 1759-60

Apschon Dragoons: Uniform red, green lining and cuff. Red breeches and green waistcoat. White button holes and buttons. Red cap turned up with green. Green saddle cloth edged white.

Nassau: Blue coat, white lapel, cuff and lining. Yellow hat lace and buttons. Yellow aiguillette and yellow loops on the lapel.

At the head of the colour plate are a fusil de dragon, an axe, carried on the off-side, a giberne or cartridge bag and the forage cap of a dragon.

The two mounted figures are, on the left, the Regiment Bourgogne and, on the right, the Regiment Mestre de Camp General. Dismounted are a cuirassier of the Regiment du Roi, a dragon of the Regiment de Saxe and an officer of the Regiment Mestre de Camp General.

FRENCH INFANTRY AT MINDEN

All coats are grey-white unless otherwise stated.

Rougergue: Red cuff and collar, grey-white breeches and waistcoat, yellow hat lace and buttons, cross pockets, three buttons on pocket and three on cuff.

La Marche: Red cuff, grey-white collar, waistcoat and breeches, yellow hat lace and buttons, cross pockets, three buttons below the pocket and two above, three on cuff.

Tournasis: Red cuff, grey-white collar, waistcoat and breeches, yellow hat lace and buttons, five buttons on pocket, four on cuff.

Touraine: Medium blue cuff, grey-white collar and breeches, medium blue waistcoat, white hat lace and buttons, vertical pockets, six buttons on pocket and four on cuff.

Belzunce: Grey-white cuff, collar, waistcoat and breeches, yellow hat lace and buttons, cross pockets, three buttons on pocket and three on cuff.

Picardie: Grey-white cuff, collar, waistcoat and breeches, yellow hat lace and buttons, vertical pocket, nine buttons on the pocket, four on the cuff.

Auvergne: Grey-white collar and breeches, violet waistcoat, white hat lace and buttons, cross pockets, three buttons on the pocket, three on the cuff.

Lowendahl: Blue coat, white cuff, collar, waistcoat and breeches, yellow hat lace and buttons, cross pockets, three buttons on the pocket, three on cuff.

Saint Germain: Blue coat, yellow cuff and collar, lapel and lining, blue waistcoat and breeches, white hat lace and buttons, cross pockets, three buttons on the pocket and three on the cuff.

Bergh: Blue coat, red cuff, collar and lapel, white waistcoat and breeches, white hat lace and buttons, cross pocket, three buttons on pocket and three on the cuff.

Condé: Red cuff, grey-white collar, waistcoat and breeches, white hat lace, yellow buttons, five buttons on pocket and five on cuff.

Enghien: Red cuff, grey-white collar, waistcoat and breeches, white hat lace and buttons, two vertical pockets, five buttons on pocket and four on the cuff.

Aquitaine: Blue cuff, grey-white collar, waistcoat and breeches, yellow hat lace and buttons, cross pockets, four buttons on pocket and four on the cuff.

Vastan: Grey-white cuff, collar, waistcoat and breeches, white hat lace, yellow buttons, two vertical pockets with four buttons, three on cuff.

Du Roi: Grey-white cuff and collar, blue waistcoat and breeches, yellow hat lace and buttons, cross pockets with three buttons, three on the cuff. There were nine buttons down the front of the coat with golden yellow loops and button holes, blue stockings, blue lining, officers had gold lace loops and button holes.

Champagne: All items grey-white. Yellow hat lace and buttons, Two vertical pockets with six buttons, four on cuff.

Piedmont: Black cuff, grey-white collar, waistcoat and breeches, yellow hat lace and buttons, shield-shaped pocket with eight buttons, three on cuff.

Dauphiné: Blue cuff, grey-white collar, waistcoat and breeches, white hat lace, yellow buttons, vertical pocket with seven buttons, five on cuff.

Nassau Saarbrücken: Blue coat and collar, red waistcoat and breeches, straw-colour cuff, white hat lace and buttons, cross pocket with three buttons, three on cuff.

French and Allied Units, 1759

The colour plate above shows a soldier of a Regiment of the Line with red facings, with next a Grenadier de France. On the right is an Artilleryman and a Fusilier of Saxon Infantry.

Royal Bavière: Blue coat, waistcoat and breeches, black cuff
and collar, white hat lace and buttons, cross pocket with four
buttons, three on cuff, white lining, white lace loops on black
lapel, waistcoat and pocket. Collar, lapel and cuff piped with
white.
Planta: Red coat, blue cuff, collar, waistcoat and breeches,
yellow hat lace and white buttons, cross pocket with three
buttons, blue lining and stockings.
Courten: Red coat and collar, blue cuff, waistcoat and breeches,
white hat lace and buttons, cross pocket with three buttons,
three on cuff, blue lining and stockings.
Grenadiers Royaux: All white uniform with blue shoulder strap,
white buttons and cocked hat.

Artillery: Blue coat, red collar, cuff and lining. Yellow hat lace
and buttons, four buttons on pocket, three on cuff.

Included in the French forces at Minden were thirteen
battalions of Saxon Infantry. The Foot Guards wore red with
yellow facings and the Line Infantry white coats with facings of
various colours.